Embracing Equality: The Journey of LGBTQ+ Rights

Table of content

Introduction

Chapter 1

Chapter 2

Chapter 3

Chapter 4

Chapter 5

Chapter 6

Chapter 7

Chapter 8

Chapter 9

Conclusion

Brief history on LGBTQ+
In 1924, human rights activist Henry Gerber founded the Society for Human Rights in the United States, which became the country's first gay rights organization. The organization aimed to break the stereotypes and taboos about homosexuality. Henry Gerber was also arrested several times because of his work.

Then in 1969, a gay bar called the Stonewall Inn in New York City was raided by police who claimed the bar was selling liquor without a license. The police forced their guests into police vans, which enraged the crowd and forced the police to barricade themselves for their protection. This incident became known as The Stonewall Riot, which attracted a lot of media coverage and brought to light the issues facing the lesbian, gay, bisexual and transgender communities. In 1970, demonstrations in support of the gay community were held in New York, Chicago, Los Angeles and San Francisco.
Colorful, uplifting float and celebrity parades, merry festivals, workshops, picnics and parties are key components of Pride Month, also known as Gay Pride, which is celebrated in June in the United States and around the world.

 Pride Month commemorates the years of struggle for civil rights and the continued pursuit of equal justice before the law for lesbian, gay, bisexual, transgender and queer communities and the achievements of lesbian, gay, bisexual and transgender people. But why is Pride Month celebrated in June?

The organized pursuit of lesbian, gay, bisexual, transgender, and contestation rights in the United States dates back at least to 1924 and the founding of the Society of Human Rights in Chicago by Henry Gerber. But the event that sparked the lesbian, gay, bisexual, transgender and questioning rights movement took place in June 1969 in New York's Greenwich Village at the Stonewall Inn. In the early hours of June 28, police raided this popular meeting place for young members of the lesbian, gay, bisexual, transgender and interrogation community - arresting staff for selling alcohol without a license, beating many of the patrons and evacuating the bar from the crowd they watched as bar patrons were angrily herded into police cars.

Previously, witnesses had passively watched police harassment of members of the lesbian, gay, bisexual, transgender and interrogation communities, but this time the crowd taunted the police and threw coins and then bottles and debris at them, forcing the police to withdraw Bar at barricade awaits reinforcements. It wasn't long before about 400 people rioted.

Although police reinforcements dispersed the crowd, rioting outside the bar waxed and waned over the next five days, and these Stonewall riots (also known as Stonewall riots) provided the spark that started the lesbian gay bisexual transgender and questioning rights movement in the United States triggered inflamed.

In the four years leading up to the Stonewall riots, Philadelphia activists staged protests outside Independence Hall on July 4 as an "annual reminder" that gays and lesbians were being denied basic civil rights. But these events were carefully restricted picket demonstrations, where men were told to dress appropriately for business, women were told to wear skirts and blouses, and public displays of affection were forbidden. At the Eastern Regional Conference of Homophile Organizations in Philadelphia on November 2, 1969, the idea of a march in response to the Stonewall events was proposed.

The procession, scheduled for June 28, 1970, the first anniversary of the Stonewall riots, was named for the street that was the epicenter of New York City's lesbian, gay, bisexual, transgender, and interrogation communities , and after the location where the procession would take place, location referred to as the Christopher Street Liberation Day March Start.

Although "Gay Power" had been proposed as a slogan for the march, it was argued that the movement still needed political empowerment but that its members took great pride in their sexual identity. Therefore it was decided that the theme of the march would be Gay Pride. Sources differ on the exact number of people who ultimately took part in the march -- estimates range from 1,000 to 20,000 -- but no one disputes that there were, at most, a few hundred protesters at the beginning.

 However, by the time the march ended 51 blocks north at Sheep Meadow in Central Park, its numbers had increased dramatically as individuals along the way joined the procession in solidarity, chanting slogans like "Say it clear, say it loud." Gay is good, Gay is proud."

The day before the Pride march in New York City, about 150 people in Chicago had wrapped up a week-long event with the country's first march to commemorate Stonewall. On the day of the New York march, "the world's first legal pro-gay parade" took place on Hollywood Boulevard in Los Angeles and a "Gay In" took place in San Francisco's Golden Gate Park.

Thereafter, in the United States, Gay Pride, Orlesbian Gay Bisexual Transgender and Questioned Pride were generally celebrated on the last Sunday in June (although there were many exceptions), when somber marches gave way to joyful celebrations. Over time, the day grew into a month-long event. It was officially recognized by the US government when President Bill Clinton declared June 1999 "Gay and Lesbian Pride Month", President Barack Obama declared June "LGBT Pride Month" and President Joe Biden declared Lesbian Respect , Gay, Bisexual and Transgender and Queer (LGBTQ+) Pride Month. Elsewhere in the world, Pride is celebrated at different times of the year, although many cities celebrate it in June.

Lesbian, Gay, Bisexual, Transgender and Queer (LGBTQ) Pride Month is currently celebrated in June each year to honor the 1969 Stonewall Uprising in Manhattan. The Stonewall Uprising was a turning point for the gay liberation movement in the United States. In the USA, the last Sunday in June was initially celebrated as "Gay Pride Day", but the actual day was flexible. In major cities across the country, the "day" soon grew into a month-long series of events.

Today, celebrations include pride parades, picnics, parties, workshops, symposiums and concerts, and LGBTQ Pride Month events attract millions of participants around the world. Memorial services will be held this month for members of the community lost to hate crime or HIV/AIDS.

The purpose of Remembrance Month is to recognize the influence that lesbian, gay, bisexual and transgender people have
had history locally, nationally and internationally.

In 1994, a coalition of educational organizations in the United States designated October as LGBT History Month. In 1995, a resolution passed by the General Assembly of the National Education Association included LGBT History Month in a list of commemorative months. National Coming Out Day (October 11) as well as the first "March on Washington" in 1979 are celebrated in the LGBTQ community during LGBT History Month.

The first Pride march in New York City was held on June 28, 1970 to mark the one-year anniversary of the Stonewall Uprising. Primary sources available at the Library of Congress provide detailed information on how this first Pride march was planned and why activists were so strongly convinced that it should exist.

Browsing the records of Lili Vincenz and Frank Kameny in the library's Manuscripts section, researchers can find planning documents, correspondence, flyers, ephemera, and more from the first Pride marches in 1970, giving the community an opportunity to gather and to commemorate riots on Christopher Street last summer, which saw thousands of homosexuals take to the streets to protest centuries of abuse... from government hostility to discrimination in employment and housing to mafia control of gay bars and Anti-Gay Laws" (Christopher Street Liberation flyer). Day Committee, Franklin Kameny Papers).

The concept behind the first Pride march came from members of the Eastern Regional Conference of Homophile Organizations (ERCHO) who had organized an annual July 4 (1965-1969) demonstration at Independence Hall in Philadelphia dubbed the "Reminder Day Pickets ' was known. At the ERCHO conference in November 1969, the 13 homophile organizations present voted to pass a resolution to organize a national annual demonstration named Christopher Street Liberation Day.

As members of the Mattachine Society of Washington, Frank Kameny and Lilli Vincenz, along with activists in New York City and other homophile groups associated with ERCHO, participated in the discussion, planning and promotion of the first Pride.

By all estimates, there were three to five thousand protesters at the first Pride in New York City, and today the number of protesters in New York City is in the millions. Since 1970, LGBTQ+ people have continued to gather in June to march with Pride and demonstrate for equality.

Pride honors the gay rights protests of the 1960s
When asked when the gay rights movement began in this country, reference is usually made to June 28, 1969: the night of the Stonewall riots. Caitlin McCarthy, the archivist at The Center, an LGBTQ+ community center in New York City, explains that the Stonewall riot was one of many.

"QTPOC-led riots like those at Stonewall and The Haven in New York, Cooper Donuts and the Black Cat Tavern in LA, and Compton's Cafeteria in San Francisco were all responses to police harassment and brutality," says McCarthy.

At the time, people perceived by police to be men could be legally arrested for engaging in drag, and people perceived by police to be women could also be arrested for sharing less than three parts wore "feminine clothing". In fact, police often raided bars looking for these alleged violations. On the summer night most people credit as the origin of Pride, patrons at the Stonewall Inn f color - fought each other away from another police raid.

The first Pride March - a rally in NYC on the last Saturday in June - was dubbed Christopher Street Liberation Day in honor of the Stonewall uprising. For context: Christopher Street is the physical home of the Stonewall Inn. "The Christopher Street Liberation Day Committee was formed to commemorate the one-year anniversary of the Stonewall riots in June 1969 with a march from the West Village followed by a 'gay be-in' gathering in Central Park," says McCarthy . This helped cement Stonewall as the most culturally recognized foundation of Pride.

Trans and non-gender people of color started with pride
Many people are familiar with the transformative activism of Marsha P. Johnson and Sylvia Rivera, McCarthy says. Johnson and Rivera co-founded STAR, the Street Transvestite Action Revolutionaries, which organized direct action such as sit-ins and provided shelter for transgender people and other homeless LGBTQ+ youth. Both activists were also members of the anti-capitalist, internationalist group Gay Liberation Front (GLF), which organized marches, hosted dances to raise funds for queer people in need, and a gay newspaper called Come Out! in 1969.

McCarthy tells Bustle that Johnson and Rivera's lesser-known (but no less important) siblings include Zazu Nova, a member of GLF and STAR; Stormé Delarverie, a drag king and emcee of trans and drag-centric touring group Jewel Box Revue; and Lani Ka'ahumanu, who founded the Bay Area Bisexual Network.

"Gay Pride" replaced "Gay Power" in the 1970s
According to a 2006 article published in American Sociological Review magazine, "gay power" was a common slogan used in queer publications and at protests in the '60s and early '70s. Many local Black Power groups and radical queer organizing groups were able to rally against police brutality in the 1970s. This collaboration makes the use of "gay power" rather unsurprising at this point.

"Radical organizing, influenced by and in concert with the anti-racist and anti-war movement, followed [Stonewall]," says McCarthy. "The protests, sit-ins and direct actions conducted and participated in by early gay liberation groups such as the Gay Liberation Front, Street Transvestite Action Revolutionaries, Dyketactics and the Combahee River Collective called for radical structural change in the face of ongoing repression."

The National Historic Landmark nomination for the Stonewall Inn, prepared for the United States Department of the Interior in 1999, also noted that "gay power" rather than "gay pride" was used in most settings. Although activist Craig Schoonmaker is often credited with popularizing the phrase "gay pride" (as opposed to power) in 1970, it is worth noting that his organizational vision excluded lesbians. Today, "pride" is used as a shorthand to refer to LGBTQ+ celebrations and protests alike.

This is what Pride Month looks like today
Despite these radical roots, corporate-sponsored Pride sunglasses and corporate logos with temporary splashes of rainbows are hallmarks of modern-day celebrations of Pride Month. Many people consider it disrespectful to Pride's history when large corporations sponsor commercialized Pride marches. However, the Stonewall riot that most people credit as the origin of Pride was a direct response to police crackdown and brutality, but Pride marches today are usually accompanied by police escorts.

However, in light of the Black Lives Matter protests of 2020, Pride organizations are reconsidering their positions on Pride policing, with some deciding to ban police officers from marching at Pride until certain racial justice reform requirements are met.

Many LGBTQ+ people find that a month of visibility of 12 is not enough to ensure the safety and justice of queer people, while others argue that even a month of rainbow flags at your local destination is better than silence. (The radical founders of the Pride movement probably wouldn't have approved of the silence, either.) Regardless of how you're celebrating Pride, knowing its history can give you a more complete experience of the month — and a deeper understanding of how it became possible.

This guide comes from the Know-How library, a tool on the Unifrog platform. Not sure whether to take the ACT or the SAT? Or how to give the perfect Oxbridge practice interview?

 The Know-How Library is an easily searchable library of hundreds of expert guides for students and teachers, covering every aspect of the development process. It is included by default for Unifrog partner sch

Sexual orientation and gender identity are fundamental aspects of human diversity and self-expression. However, they are often misunderstood or confused due to societal norms, stereotypes, and limited awareness. This note aims to provide a basic understanding of sexual orientation and gender identity, emphasizing the importance of respect, acceptance, and inclusivity.

Sexual Orientation:

Sexual orientation refers to a person's enduring pattern of emotional, romantic, and sexual attractions to individuals of the same gender (homosexuality), opposite gender (heterosexuality), or multiple genders (bisexuality, pansexuality). It is an innate and deeply personal aspect of one's identity. Sexual orientation exists along a diverse spectrum, with individuals experiencing a range of attractions and identities.

Gender Identity:

Gender identity pertains to an individual's deeply-felt sense of being male, female, or something beyond the binary concept of gender. It may not necessarily align with the sex assigned at birth. Gender identity is internally felt and self-defined, and individuals may identify as transgender, non-binary, genderqueer, or other gender identities. It is crucial to respect and affirm people's gender identities and use appropriate pronouns according to their self-identification.

Distinction between Sexual Orientation and Gender Identity:

It is important to note that sexual orientation and gender identity are distinct aspects of a person's identity. Sexual orientation relates to who one is attracted to, while gender identity refers to one's internal sense of self. A person's sexual orientation can be independent of their gender identity. For example, a transgender person may identify as heterosexual, homosexual, bisexual, or any other sexual orientation, just like cisgender individuals.

Fluidity and Diversity:

Sexual orientation and gender identity are fluid and diverse, with individuals experiencing different attractions and identities throughout their lives. It is crucial to recognize and respect this diversity, understanding that everyone's journey of self-discovery and self-expression is unique.

Importance of Acceptance and Inclusivity:

Understanding sexual orientation and gender identity is crucial for fostering acceptance, inclusivity, and equality for LGBTQ+ individuals. By educating ourselves and challenging stereotypes and prejudices, we can create environments that respect and affirm people of all sexual orientations and gender identities. It is essential to listen to and amplify LGBTQ+ voices, support advocacy efforts, and work towards dismantling discriminatory practices and policies.

Chapter 2

The Evolution of LGBTQ+ Rights Movements

The fight for LGBTQ+ rights has been a long and arduous journey, marked by significant milestones, challenges, and triumphs. The evolution of LGBTQ+ rights movements reflects the tireless efforts of activists and allies who have fought for equality, acceptance, and justice. This note explores the key phases and pivotal moments in the history of LGBTQ+ rights movements.

Pre-Stonewall Era: Early Activism
Before the pivotal Stonewall Uprising in 1969, LGBTQ+ activism existed, albeit on a smaller scale. LGBTQ+ individuals and allies formed organizations and advocacy groups to challenge discrimination and societal stigma. Notable pioneers such as Harry Hay, Barbara Gittings, and Frank Kameny laid the groundwork for future movements.

The Stonewall Uprising and Its Impact
The Stonewall Uprising, which erupted in response to police raids on the Stonewall Inn in New York City, marked a turning point in LGBTQ+ activism. The spontaneous protests and clashes with law enforcement ignited a spirit of resistance and solidarity within the community. The event galvanized the formation of LGBTQ+ organizations and the emergence of broader movements for civil rights.

Milestones in LGBTQ+ Activism
In the wake of Stonewall, significant milestones were achieved in the fight for LGBTQ+ rights.

The early 1970s witnessed the establishment of LGBTQ+ pride parades, marking a celebration of identity and visibility. The American Psychiatric Association's removal of homosexuality from the list of mental disorders in 1973 was a crucial step towards destigmatization.

The 1980s and 1990s were marked by the devastating impact of the HIV/AIDS epidemic, which prompted widespread activism and community support.

Chapter 3

Legal frameworks play a crucial role in safeguarding the rights and well-being of LGBTQ+ individuals around the world. Over the years, significant progress has been made in establishing legal protections and recognition for sexual orientation and gender identity. However, challenges and disparities persist, and the struggle for full equality continues. This note explores the importance of legal frameworks and their impact on LGBTQ+ rights.

Decriminalization of Homosexuality:

The decriminalization of consensual same-sex relationships is a fundamental step toward ensuring LGBTQ+ rights. Many countries have abolished laws that criminalized homosexuality, contributing to a more inclusive society. However, some nations still enforce discriminatory legislation, leading to human rights abuses and persecution.

Anti-Discrimination Laws and Policies:

Anti-discrimination laws protect LGBTQ+ individuals from prejudice and bias in various aspects of life, including employment, housing, education, healthcare, and public services. These laws aim to eliminate discrimination based on sexual orientation and gender identity, promoting equal opportunities and social inclusion.

Recognition of Same-Sex Relationships:

The legal recognition of same-sex relationships grants LGBTQ+ couples the same rights and benefits as heterosexual couples. Marriage equality, civil unions, and domestic partnerships provide legal protections, such as inheritance rights, healthcare decision-making, and access to spousal benefits. While progress has been made in many jurisdictions, disparities persist globally.

Adoption and Parenting Rights:

Ensuring LGBTQ+ individuals and couples have equal rights to adopt and become parents is crucial for family formation and protection. Legal frameworks addressing adoption and parenting rights help create inclusive and diverse family structures, promoting the well-being of children and providing legal security for LGBTQ+ parents.

Transgender Rights and Legal Recognition:

Transgender rights involve legal recognition of gender identity and protection against discrimination. Legal frameworks vary worldwide, with some countries allowing gender marker changes on identification documents, providing access to healthcare and gender-affirming treatments, and protecting transgender individuals from discrimination and violence.

Challenges and Ongoing Struggles:

Despite progress in legal frameworks, challenges persist in achieving full LGBTQ+ equality. Some regions lack comprehensive legal protections, leading to discrimination, violence, and marginalization. Transgender rights, in particular, face significant hurdles, including challenges in legal gender recognition and healthcare access. Ongoing advocacy and legal reforms are essential to address these disparities.

It is important to note that legal frameworks alone cannot create societal change; they must be accompanied by education, awareness, and cultural shifts. Additionally, the intersectionality of LGBTQ+ identities with race, ethnicity, religion, and other factors must be considered to ensure inclusive and equitable legal protections for all individuals within the community.

The fight for LGBTQ+ rights is an ongoing global struggle, with progress made through the dedication and advocacy of LGBTQ+ activists, allies, and organizations. Continued efforts to establish and strengthen legal frameworks are vital to achieving full equality and societal acceptance for LGBTQ+ individuals worldwide.

Chapter 4

Social Stigma and Discrimination

Social stigma and discrimination are significant barriers faced by LGBTQ+ individuals worldwide. Despite advancements in legal protections and increased visibility, many LGBTQ+ people continue to experience prejudice, bias, and exclusion based on their sexual orientation or gender identity.

This note explores the nature and impact of social stigma and discrimination and emphasizes the importance of challenging these harmful attitudes and practices.

Social stigma refers to the negative beliefs, attitudes, and stereotypes that society attaches to a particular group or identity. In the context of LGBTQ+ individuals, social stigma arises from deeply ingrained societal norms, religious beliefs, and cultural biases that label non-heterosexual orientations and non-cisgender identities as deviant or abnormal.

This stigma often leads to discriminatory behaviors and practices that can manifest in various ways, including verbal abuse, exclusion, physical violence, and institutionalized discrimination.

The consequences of social stigma and discrimination on LGBTQ+ individuals are profound and far-reaching. Stigmatizing attitudes contribute to higher rates of mental health issues such as depression, anxiety, and suicidal ideation among LGBTQ+ individuals.

 The fear of rejection and discrimination often forces individuals to conceal their identities, leading to a diminished sense of self and increased feelings of isolation and shame. Stigmatization also hinders access to essential services such as healthcare, employment, housing, and education, perpetuating systemic inequalities and limiting opportunities for LGBTQ+ people to thrive.

To address social stigma and discrimination, it is crucial to foster widespread education and awareness about sexual orientation and gender identity.

This includes promoting LGBTQ+-inclusive curricula in schools, providing comprehensive training for healthcare professionals, and encouraging open dialogue in communities. Challenging stereotypes and misconceptions through media representation and storytelling can also play a pivotal role in shifting public perceptions and fostering empathy and understanding.

Legislation and policies that protect LGBTQ+ individuals from discrimination are fundamental in dismantling social stigma. Efforts to advocate for comprehensive anti-discrimination laws and equal rights are necessary to create a more inclusive society. Additionally, establishing support networks, community organizations, and safe spaces for LGBTQ+ individuals can provide vital resources, solidarity, and a sense of belonging.

As allies and individuals, it is essential to confront our own biases, challenge discriminatory behavior, and actively promote acceptance and equality. This includes using inclusive language, respecting individuals' chosen names and pronouns, and amplifying LGBTQ+ voices and experiences. By fostering an environment of acceptance and respect, we can contribute to a society that celebrates diversity and dismantles the harmful effects of social stigma and discrimination faced by the LGBTQ+ community.

Chapter 5

Mental health is an essential aspect of overall well-being for individuals across all communities, and the LGBTQ+ community is no exception. Members of the LGBTQ+ (Lesbian, Gay, Bisexual, Transgender, Queer/Questioning, and others) community often face unique challenges and stressors that can impact their mental health. It is crucial to address these issues and provide support and resources to promote their psychological well-being.

One significant factor affecting mental health in LGBTQ+ communities is the presence of stigma, discrimination, and prejudice. LGBTQ+ individuals may experience societal bias, rejection, or even violence due to their sexual orientation, gender identity, or expression. This can lead to increased levels of stress, anxiety, depression, and other mental health conditions. It is important to create inclusive and accepting environments that validate the experiences and identities of LGBTQ+ individuals, reducing the negative impact of discrimination on their mental health.

Another aspect that can influence mental health is the process of coming out. Coming out is a deeply personal journey that involves revealing one's sexual orientation or gender identity to others. While it can be a liberating and empowering experience, it can also be accompanied by fear, anxiety, and uncertainty. Supportive networks, including friends, family, and LGBTQ+ organizations, can play a vital role in fostering positive mental health outcomes during this process.

Access to mental health services is crucial for LGBTQ+ individuals, as they may face unique challenges in finding affirming and knowledgeable providers. Healthcare providers need to be sensitive to the specific needs and experiences of LGBTQ+ individuals, ensuring they receive respectful and inclusive care. Culturally competent mental health professionals who are aware of the issues faced by the community can provide appropriate support and therapy.

Intersectionality is another important consideration in understanding mental health within LGBTQ+ communities. Individuals who belong to multiple marginalized groups, such as LGBTQ+ people of color or LGBTQ+ individuals with disabilities, may face compounded discrimination and challenges. Recognizing and addressing these intersecting identities is vital to providing inclusive and comprehensive mental health support.

Supportive interventions and resources can significantly contribute to improving mental health outcomes for LGBTQ+ individuals.

This includes creating safe spaces, such as LGBTQ+ community centers or support groups, where individuals can connect with others who share similar experiences. Online platforms and helplines specifically catering to LGBTQ+ communities can also provide valuable mental health resources and counseling.

Education and awareness campaigns play a crucial role in challenging stigmas and promoting understanding of LGBTQ+ mental health. By fostering empathy and acceptance within society, we can help create an environment that supports the mental well-being of all individuals, irrespective of their sexual orientation or gender identity.

Chapter 6

LGBTQ+ (Lesbian, Gay, Bisexual, Transgender, Queer/Questioning, and others) youth face unique challenges within educational settings. It is crucial for educators, administrators, and policymakers to create inclusive and supportive environments that prioritize the well-being and educational success of LGBTQ+ students. This note aims to highlight the importance of addressing the specific needs and experiences of LGBTQ+ youth in education.

Firstly, it is essential to recognize that LGBTQ+ youth often face higher rates of bullying, harassment, and discrimination compared to their heterosexual and cisgender peers.

This can have detrimental effects on their mental health, self-esteem, and educational outcomes. Educators must actively work to create safe spaces within schools where LGBTQ+ students can feel accepted, supported, and valued.

Inclusive policies and practices play a significant role in supporting LGBTQ+ youth. Schools should adopt anti-bullying and anti-discrimination policies that explicitly include sexual orientation, gender identity, and gender expression.

These policies should be widely communicated and enforced consistently to ensure the well-being of LGBTQ+ students. Additionally, schools should provide access to gender-neutral facilities, such as restrooms and changing areas, to accommodate the needs of transgender and gender-nonconforming students.

Curriculum inclusivity is another vital aspect of supporting LGBTQ+ youth in education. Including LGBTQ+ history, literature, and contributions within the curriculum helps foster a more comprehensive understanding of society and promotes acceptance.

LGBTQ+-inclusive sex education that addresses diverse sexual orientations, gender identities, and relationships is also essential for the well-being and safety of LGBTQ+ youth.

Supportive resources and support systems within schools are critical for LGBTQ+ youth. Establishing LGBTQ+ student clubs, such as gay-straight alliances or gender-sexuality alliances, provides a platform for students to connect with peers and create a sense of community. Trained counselors or support staff who are knowledgeable about LGBTQ+ issues can offer guidance and support to students, ensuring their emotional well-being is prioritized.

Professional development for educators is crucial to create a welcoming and inclusive learning environment. Training sessions that address LGBTQ+ cultural competence, inclusive language, and strategies to prevent and address bullying and discrimination can equip teachers with the necessary tools to support LGBTQ+ students effectively. Educators should also familiarize themselves with local and national resources that provide support and guidance on LGBTQ+ issues.

Collaboration with families and caregivers is key to creating a supportive educational environment for LGBTQ+ youth. Schools can engage in open and respectful communication with parents and guardians to address concerns, provide resources, and ensure that the needs of LGBTQ+ students are understood and met.

Chapter 7

The intersection of religion, culture, and LGBTQ+ rights is a complex and multifaceted topic that requires careful exploration and understanding.

Throughout history, religious and cultural beliefs have influenced societal attitudes towards sexual orientation and gender identity, often posing challenges to the advancement of LGBTQ+ rights. However, it is essential to recognize that progress is being made as religious and cultural perspectives continue to evolve and become more inclusive.

Religion and culture have a significant influence on the values, norms, and moral frameworks that shape individuals' perceptions and attitudes towards LGBTQ+ individuals. In some religious and cultural contexts, there may be teachings or interpretations that view homosexuality, bisexuality, or transgender identities as sinful or immoral.

These beliefs can lead to discrimination, stigmatization, and marginalization of LGBTQ+ individuals within their religious or cultural communities.

However, it is important to note that religious and cultural beliefs are diverse and multifaceted, and not all adherents of a particular religion or cultural group hold negative views towards LGBTQ+ individuals. Many religious and cultural traditions emphasize compassion, acceptance, and love, providing spaces for inclusive interpretations and practices.

Over time, there has been a growing movement within various religious and cultural communities to affirm and support LGBTQ+ individuals. Religious leaders, theologians, and scholars have engaged in dialogues and reinterpretations of scriptures or sacred texts to foster a more inclusive understanding of sexual orientation and gender identity. Progressive religious and cultural organizations have emerged, advocating for LGBTQ+ rights and challenging discriminatory practices.

The struggle for LGBTQ+ rights within religious and cultural contexts often involves navigating a complex landscape of reconciling one's sexual orientation or gender identity with deeply held religious or cultural beliefs. Many LGBTQ+ individuals seek to find a balance between their identities and their faith or cultural heritage, often working towards affirming and inclusive spaces within their communities.

Additionally, alliances and collaborations between LGBTQ+ advocacy organizations and religious or cultural groups are increasingly common. These partnerships aim to promote dialogue, understanding, and acceptance, challenging the notion that religious and cultural identities are inherently in conflict with LGBTQ+ rights. They work towards fostering spaces of inclusion, providing support for LGBTQ+ individuals, and advocating for policies that protect their rights.

It is crucial to recognize that the promotion of LGBTQ+ rights within religious and cultural contexts is not a monolithic process. Different religions, denominations, and cultural communities have diverse beliefs and practices, and progress towards LGBTQ+ inclusion varies across these groups. Respectful dialogue, education, and engagement are vital in fostering understanding and promoting acceptance within religious and cultural communities.

Chapter 8

The fight for LGBTQ+ rights is a global struggle, with progress and challenges varying significantly across countries and regions. International perspectives on LGBTQ+ rights provide valuable insight into the diverse legal frameworks, cultural attitudes, and ongoing efforts to promote equality and inclusion for LGBTQ+ individuals worldwide.

While some countries have made significant strides in advancing LGBTQ+ rights, others continue to criminalize same-sex relationships or deny legal recognition to gender identities beyond the binary. Understanding these international perspectives is crucial for fostering dialogue, identifying best practices, and advocating for change on a global scale.

Legal frameworks and protections for LGBTQ+ individuals vary widely across nations. Several countries have implemented comprehensive anti-discrimination laws, recognizing sexual orientation and gender identity as protected categories. These legal protections aim to ensure equal rights and opportunities in areas such as employment, housing, education, and healthcare.

Marriage equality is another area where international perspectives diverge. As of now, a growing number of countries have legalized same-sex marriage, granting LGBTQ+ couples the same rights and recognition as heterosexual couples. However, many nations still deny same-sex couples the right to marry or have varying degrees of legal recognition, such as civil partnerships or registered partnerships.

Transgender rights and legal recognition of gender identity also exhibit significant disparities worldwide. Some countries have adopted progressive measures, allowing individuals to legally change their gender marker and access gender-affirming healthcare. In contrast, others lack formal legal recognition or impose burdensome requirements for gender reassignment procedures.

Cultural attitudes and societal acceptance play a significant role in shaping LGBTQ+ rights internationally. While some countries have witnessed a remarkable shift towards greater acceptance and inclusivity, others continue to grapple with deep-rooted prejudices and discriminatory attitudes. Societal acceptance is influenced by factors such as religion, tradition, education, and exposure to diverse perspectives.

International perspectives on LGBTQ+ rights also highlight the intersectionality of identities and the varying experiences of marginalized LGBTQ+ communities. LGBTQ+ individuals who belong to racial and ethnic minorities, indigenous communities, or other marginalized groups may face compounded discrimination and unique challenges. Understanding and addressing these intersecting identities is crucial for promoting inclusive and comprehensive LGBTQ+ rights globally.

Advocacy and international organizations play a pivotal role in promoting LGBTQ+ rights worldwide. Non-governmental organizations, human rights groups, and grassroots movements tirelessly work to challenge discriminatory laws, provide support to LGBTQ+ communities, and advocate for legal and social change. International organizations like the United Nations and regional bodies contribute to the conversation by addressing LGBTQ+ rights within their frameworks and encouraging member states to uphold and protect these rights.

International perspectives on LGBTQ+ rights highlight the ongoing challenges faced by LGBTQ+ individuals in many parts of the world, including violence, persecution, and social exclusion. However, they also offer hope and inspiration by showcasing successful campaigns, legal victories, and social progress in promoting equality and human rights. By understanding these diverse perspectives, we can foster dialogue, support local initiatives, and collaborate globally to create a more inclusive and equitable world for all LGBTQ+ individuals.

Chapter 9

As we look toward the future, it is essential to recognize the challenges and opportunities that lie ahead in the pursuit of equality and inclusivity for the LGBTQ+ community. While significant progress has been made in advancing LGBTQ+ rights, there is still work to be done to ensure the full realization of equality and the protection of human rights for all individuals, regardless of their sexual orientation or gender identity.

One of the key challenges is the persistence of discrimination and prejudice against the LGBTQ+ community. Despite legal advancements, LGBTQ+ individuals continue to face social stigma, exclusion, and even violence in various parts of the world. Combating discrimination requires ongoing efforts to challenge societal attitudes, promote education and awareness, and enact and enforce comprehensive anti-discrimination laws.

Transgender rights remain an important focus in the fight for LGBTQ+ equality. Transgender and gender-diverse individuals face unique challenges, including barriers to legal recognition, limited access to gender-affirming healthcare, and high rates of discrimination and violence. Ensuring comprehensive legal protections, improving healthcare access, and fostering inclusivity and acceptance are critical steps toward advancing transgender rights.

Healthcare disparities within the LGBTQ+ community also require attention. LGBTQ+ individuals often face barriers to accessing culturally competent and affirming healthcare services. Disparities in mental healthcare, HIV prevention and treatment, and transgender healthcare must be addressed through policies that prioritize inclusive practices, provider training, and increased research and funding.

Non-binary and gender non-conforming identities are gaining increased recognition, presenting both challenges and opportunities. Legal systems and societal norms often struggle to accommodate non-binary identities, leading to a lack of legal recognition and limited options for official documentation. Advocating for legal recognition, creating inclusive policies, and promoting education and acceptance of non-binary identities are vital steps forward.

Intersectionality remains an important consideration in advancing LGBTQ+ rights. LGBTQ+ individuals who belong to marginalized communities face compounded discrimination and unique challenges. It is crucial to address the specific needs of LGBTQ+ people of color, religious minorities, disabled individuals, and others, to ensure that their voices are heard and their rights are protected within both the LGBTQ+ movement and broader social justice initiatives.

The digital landscape presents opportunities for connectivity and community building, but it also poses challenges. Online platforms can be a double-edged sword, offering spaces for support and activism while also enabling the spread of hate speech and online harassment. Balancing free expression with efforts to combat online discrimination and protect vulnerable individuals requires ongoing dialogue and collaboration between tech companies, policymakers, and LGBTQ+ communities.

Inclusive education and comprehensive sexuality education remain critical tools for promoting acceptance and reducing prejudice. Education systems should strive to provide accurate and age-appropriate information about sexual orientation, gender identity, and diverse family structures. Implementing inclusive curricula, training educators on LGBTQ+ issues, and fostering safe and inclusive school environments are crucial steps toward creating a more accepting society.

Looking forward, it is essential to maintain and expand the alliances and coalitions that have been built between LGBTQ+ organizations and other social justice movements. Collaborative efforts that address the intersections of LGBTQ+ rights with racial justice, gender equality, disability rights, and other movements can strengthen the collective push for societal change.

Ultimately, the challenges and opportunities that lie ahead require continued activism, advocacy, and support from individuals, organizations, and policymakers. By acknowledging and addressing these challenges, we can seize the opportunities to create a future that embraces diversity, equality, and inclusion for all members of the LGBTQ+ community and ensure a society where everyone can thrive authentically and without fear of discrimination.

Conclusion:

The fight for LGBTQ+ rights has come a long way, marked by significant progress and transformative social change. The journey has been arduous, with courageous individuals and dedicated organizations tirelessly advocating for equality, acceptance, and the protection of human rights. While there have been notable victories, it is important to recognize that the struggle for full LGBTQ+ equality is ongoing.

Throughout history, LGBTQ+ individuals have faced discrimination, persecution, and marginalization. However, the resilience and determination of the LGBTQ+ community, along with their allies, have paved the way for significant legal advancements and shifts in societal attitudes. The decriminalization of homosexuality, the recognition of same-sex marriage, and the implementation of anti-discrimination laws in many countries are testament to the progress made in securing LGBTQ+ rights.

Nevertheless, challenges persist. LGBTQ+ individuals continue to face discrimination, prejudice, and violence in various parts of the world.
Transgender and gender-diverse individuals face unique barriers to recognition, healthcare, and acceptance. Intersectionality adds complexity, as the experiences of LGBTQ+ individuals from marginalized communities require specific attention and targeted support.

Looking forward, it is crucial to maintain momentum in the pursuit of LGBTQ+ rights. Inclusive policies, legislation, and legal protections must be enacted and enforced to ensure equality and non-discrimination.

 Education and awareness campaigns should continue to challenge stereotypes, combat prejudice, and foster acceptance. Mental healthcare services must be accessible and inclusive, addressing the specific needs of LGBTQ+ individuals. Collaboration and solidarity with other social justice movements are essential to achieving a more just and equitable society for all.

Support from allies is pivotal. By standing together, advocating for LGBTQ+ rights, and amplifying marginalized voices, we can create a culture that embraces diversity, celebrates differences, and affirms the inherent worth and dignity of every individual. Solidarity and empathy help break down barriers and create spaces where LGBTQ+ individuals can live authentically, free from fear and discrimination.

The journey toward LGBTQ+ equality is not yet complete, but the progress made thus far serves as inspiration and motivation to continue the work. Each step forward brings us closer to a future where every LGBTQ+ person can live their lives openly, without fear of reprisal, and where their rights are protected and respected. By joining forces, celebrating diversity, and advocating for change, we can build a world that truly embraces and affirms the rights and well-being of all individuals, regardless of their sexual orientation or gender identity.